Agricultural Notes On Hertfordshire

James Charles Clutterbuck

In the interest of creating a more extensive selection of rare historical book reprints, we have chosen to reproduce this title even though it may possibly have occasional imperfections such as missing and blurred pages, missing text, poor pictures, markings, dark backgrounds and other reproduction issues beyond our control. Because this work is culturally important, we have made it available as a part of our commitment to protecting, preserving and promoting the world's literature. Thank you for your understanding.

AGRICULTURAL NOTES

ON

HERTFORDSHIRE.

BY

THE REV. J. CLUTTERBUCK.

LONDON.
MDCCCLXIV.

FROM THE
JOURNAL OF THE ROYAL AGRICULTURAL SOCIETY OF ENGLAND,
VOL. XXV., PART II.

AGRICULTURAL NOTES

ON

HERTFORDSHIRE.

Agricultural Literature—Climate—Rainfall and Percolation of Water as tested by Dalton's Gauge—Area and Population — Sales of Fat Stock — Physical Geography—Influence of Swallow-holes on Drainage and Water Supply —The Water-level in the Chalk—Sheep Farm at Wheathampstead—The Chalk district — Irrigation — Paper-Mills — Drainage of low Meadows — Water-Cresses — Cherry-Orchards — Woods — Straw-Plait—Seed Wheats —The Bennington Flock — Heavy Roller with revolving Shafts.

Agricultural Literature.

The agriculture of Herts has already been chronicled by Ellis of Little Gaddesden (quoted by A. Young), in 1732; by Walker, in his 'Report prepared for the Board of Agriculture,' in 1759; by Clutterbuck, in his History of this county (1815); but especially by Arthur Young, in his 'Report,' published in 1804.

To that distinguished pioneer in agriculture we are indebted for our only reliable means of contrasting the agriculture of the 18th with that of the 19th century. Of him it has been well said: "If great zeal, indefatigable exertion, and an unsparing expense in making experiments can give a man a claim to the gratitude of agriculturists, Arthur Young deserved it more than most men. We will not assert that in all cases his conclusions were sound or his judgment unimpeachable, but even his blunders, if he committed any, have tended to the benefit of agriculture by exciting discussion and criticism." [*]

The above passage aptly characterises his 'Report of Herts,' which mainly embodies the opinions of the leading farmers,

---

[*] *Vide* Kirwin, 'Irish Transactions.'

amateur or professional, of that day. Drill husbandry, the cultivation of the Swede turnip, the substitution of the Southdown for the long-legged Wiltshire sheep, were then leading subjects for discussion; and it is remarkable that the introduction of improved implements and practice rests throughout this Report with amateurs, whilst the management of the most common and essential operations of husbandry in the present day will be found to be completely at variance with that of some of the best practical farmers who gave information to Arthur Young.

The name of Mr. T. Greg, of Coles, near Westmill, often quoted by A. Young, deserves a passing notice. Prompted by Mr. Coke's (Lord Leicester's) example, Mr. Greg first undertook, by the aid of Hill's scarifier, to apply to his own wet tenacious clays the principles of Norfolk husbandry. He abolished the bare summer fallow, ploughing but once for a crop, and that only in winter, using the scarifier, the drill, and the horse-hoe freely to complete his operations.

In proof that improvements in husbandry were early introduced into Hertfordshire, A. Young, quoting Mr. Rooper, of Berkhampstead, says that clover and turnips were supposed to have been introduced by Oliver Cromwell, who "gave a farmer named How a 100*l*. a year on that account," and that there had been little change in the course of cropping for one hundred years.

The climate of England, though it may have undergone some changes, must be essentially the same as when Fuller said of Hertfordshire, "It is the Garden of England for delight; men commonly say that such as buy a house in Hertfordshire, pay two years' purchase for the aire thereof;"—a salubrity due to the geological condition of the greater part of the county, gravel upon chalk.

RAINFALL AND PERCOLATION OF WATER.

The following tables of rainfall and mean temperature were kindly furnished by those gentlemen by whom the registry has been kept. The column Dalton's Gauge, under the head "Hemel Hempstead," refers to a rain-gauge, suggested by Dr. Dalton and kept at Apsley Mills for twenty-nine years last past, which only registers that portion of the rainfall which percolates 3 feet of soil. Its construction is described in 'Ree's Cyclopædia' under the head Evaporation. It is calculated that the amount so collected represents the quantity which sinks through the surface soil to the springs, which supply the rivers and give power to the mills.

The average rainfall registered for 29 years is 22·5, percolation 7·5 inches. The Table shows 25·8 of rainfall and 4·9 percolation for the last 10 years. It will be seen that the amount of rainfall increases with the longitude westward.

	Berkhampstead.		Hemel Hempstead.		Royston.	
	Longitude W. .... 0° 34′ 0″ Latitude ...... 52° 45′ 0″ Height above sea, 370 feet.		Longitude W. 0° 27′ 50″ Latitude .. 52° 45′ 0″ Height above sea, 250 feet.		Longitude W. 0° 0′ 2″ Latitude .. 52° 2′ 40″ Height above sea, 266 feet.	
Years.	Rain.	Mean Temperature.	Rain.	Dalton's Gauge.	Rain.	Mean Temperature.
1854	24·0	..	18·2	1·4	18·1	49·2
1855	30·5	45·6	25·8	5·4	25·0	46·7
1856	30·0	47·7	26·6	7·4	21·9	48·8
1857	29·2	49·6	28·1	7·4	27·9	50·5
1858	22·5	48·3	20·5	3·2	20·4	48·9
1859	33·0	49·3	32·6	4·5	25·4	50·2
1860	36·2	45·7	34·2	12·1	29·5	46·0
1861	24·1	48·0	22·2	6·4	19·8	48·5
1862	29·5	48·4	27·4	8·0	23·9	48·5
1863	26·7	49·0	22·7	3·3	17·8	49·4
Average	28·5	47·1	25·8	5·9	22·9	48·6

AREA AND POPULATION.

The geographical extent of the county may be taken to be, in length, south-west to north-east, 36 miles; south-east to north-west, 26 miles; with a circumference of from 130 to 140 miles. Halley is quoted as estimating its superficial area at 451,000 acres. The population returns 1861 give it at 391,141 acres. Clutterbuck gives the population, in 1801, 97,577; 1811, 111,654: increase, 14,077. The last returns, 1851, 167,298; 1861, 173,294: increase, 5996. Total increase since 1801, 75,717. The persons employed chiefly in agriculture in 1801 are 20,611. The families so employed in 1811, 16,998.

MARKETS AND SALES BY AUCTION.

Of the old markets, suffice it to say, that there are 18 market towns in which the old system of selling wheat by the load of 5 bushels is still very generally followed. Barnet fair is still famous for its supply of neat cattle, brought from Wales and Scotland, &c.

The modern practice of holding sales of fat stock by auction at such towns as Hitchin, Hertford, Bishop's Stortford, and

Watford, has assumed such large and increasing proportions that it may be well to trace its development as exhibited in the town of Hitchin. These sales which were here first held occasionally in 1852, took place in 1853 twice or three times in a month, and ultimately, in 1862, every week. A yard specially fitted for the purpose was opened by Messrs. Page and Harding, 8th December, 1862. Their sales in 1861 realised 65,345*l*. 4*s*.; in 1862, 79,496*l*. 5*s*.; in 1863, 107,014*l*. 0*s*. 6*d*. The sale of Christmas last, December 15, realised 5,118*l*. 9*s*., and consisted of 108 oxen, 675 sheep, 2 calves, and 44 pigs. In the year 1863: 1876 oxen, 22,492 sheep, 123 calves, 2707 pigs, and 1156 lambs were sold.

Physical Geography.

The boundaries of this county are not, as is sometimes the case, determined by the physical features. On the north, the boundary is generally coincident with the escarpment of the chalk or Chiltern range of hills; on the south-east it is formed by the Lea and its affluent the Stort; to the south it lies very much along the high ridge, where the London clay is partially capped by drift of the Eocene beds; and on the west it follows the ridge overhanging the valley of the Bulborne, in which the Grand Junction Canal finds its course. Thus the agriculture of Hertfordshire in some cases takes its character from the several counties by which it is surrounded, and from which it is divided by an ill-defined and arbitrary line. The geological features of this county are comparatively simple. It comprehends within its limits a considerable portion of the north-western limb of the chalk-basin of London. Here nearly the whole substratum is chalk, the surface of which is either covered with drift gravel, or the tertiary deposits of the London and Plastic clay; a very small part consists of the Gault clay, which, with a trace of the upper green sand, crops out from beneath the chalk.

As the physical features of the surface are necessarily ruled by the geological condition, there is a considerable sameness in the outward aspect of the county, though there is a frequent and marked difference in the nature and quality of the soils.

Speaking generally, the county may be divided into the clay and chalk districts; the former forming the southern portion adjoining the county of Middlesex; the latter extending from the outcrop of the clays to the escarpment of the chalk hills, the frontier of the counties of Buckingham, Bedford, and Cambridge. The rivers Coln and Lea flowing in opposite directions in part of their course, form a sort of natural division between these two districts, though they do not strictly determine the limits on either side.

In the southern district, the London Clay, is mostly marked by low, rounded undulations, broken by tortuous watercourses, which provide the natural escape for surface-water, and a ready outfall for artificial drainage.

SWALLOW-HOLES.

The upper levels are very frequently covered with beds of gravel, which retain a certain quantity of water for the supply of shallow wells, which, as on Bushey Heath, attract a considerable population. The water also finds vent in land-springs at the junction of the gravel with the clay, the feeders of the brooks which run into the rivers Coln and Lea. Occasionally these waters pass, in their course towards the valley, the outcrop of the sand which underlies the clay beds of the Plastic clay formation; it then sinks by swallow or "swilly holes" into the subjacent chalk, and goes directly to augment the springs whence the rivers derive their perennial sources. Very large volumes of water so sink into the earth, and the mischief which would arise from the flooding of these brooks in winter is thus much abated. It has been suggested by very high authority that the perennial supply of water to rivers might be materially augmented if artificial means were used to facilitate the absorption of these waters. Very remarkable instances of this natural drainage may be seen more or less along the outcrop of the sand beds of the Plastic clay formation in the parishes of Bushey and Aldenham. In the watercourse which leads from the reservoir at Elstree, it has been found necessary to stop these swallow-holes to prevent waste.

The construction of artificial swallow-holes deserves our consideration as a means both of maintaining a perennial supply of water to our rivers, and also of facilitating drainage operations on a system suggested more than a century ago by Elkington.

The soil of the upper levels of the clay district marked by the rounded flint-pebbles embedded in the sand is wet and unkindly, not capable of bearing grass of any value, and ungrateful under the most liberal treatment as arable land. This gravel, with its characteristic blue-pebble, is transported in many cases below the higher levels, where the sterility of the soil is in proportion to the thickness of the bed. Where the London clay comes to the surface it forms a stubborn soil, which, however, by draining and a liberal treatment is made to grow abundant crops of grass. It also favours the luxuriant growth of oak, elm, and ash timber.

Immediately beneath the London, the Plastic clay crops out. The upper or clay-beds of this formation, as the name implies, are well suited for the manufacture of kiln-ware; it is more tenacious, and less manageable than the London clay; and usually forms a narrow band on the slopes and escarpments of the hill-sides; the lower beds are of very pure sand, sometimes perfectly white, suited for domestic, horticultural, and other purposes, though some of the beds are interspersed with rolled pebbles. To the breaking up of this stratum much of the soil that covers the chalk is due, and from hence the hard conglomerate known as Hertfordshire pudding-stone is derived. The most fertile spots in this district are found at the outcrop of these strata, where the clay and sand are amalgamated so as to form a friable and kindly soil. The geological condition here described extends more or less in a band across the county from Moor Park, near Rickmansworth, on the west, to its eastern limit bounded by the river Stort.

The neighbourhood of Bishops Stortford furnishes a good example of farming under geological conditions not found elsewhere in this county, but resembling those which subsist in some parts of Essex. The river Stort runs through a trough in the chalk, over which the Plastic clay-formation crops out on the side of the valley. Its beds of clay and sand here amalgamate with the flint-gravel, with which the chalk is covered on the lower levels, to form a light, friable, and fertile soil, suited to four-course husbandry. On the higher levels the tertiary clay forms rather wide-spread "plateaus," covered very generally with a drift consisting of water-worn chalk, with some chalk-flints. This drift, for such it appears to be, is not found in the western parts of the clay-districts of Hertfordshire under the same geological conditions of subsoil, though it is very extensively diffused in Essex, where it presents some of the best cornland in that county. It would be very interesting to trace the extent of this deposit in both counties, and, if possible, account for its unusual presence as a covering to the tertiary beds resting on the chalk.

The Water-level in the Chalk.

As in the case of the clays, the chalk-district may be sub-divided; it has been so treated by Arthur Young, who, in his maps, lays down the principal part as loam, distinguishing as chalk only that small space which is drained by rivers running to the north with a fall anticlinal to the natural dip of the stratum. Adopting this division, of which it would be difficult to define the exact limits, we find that the southern slope from the northern limits of the county to the point where the river

Coln enters the county of Middlesex, has a total dip of about 350 feet, or from the higher ground in Bedfordshire of 650 feet, which latter point is about 770 feet above the level of the sea. The highest ground on the ridges between the rivers is capped with portions of the plastic clay *in situ*, which may be deemed outlying patches of the clay-district, in some cases covered with gravel to a sufficient depth to retain the water to serve the ordinary wants of villages or hamlets, such as Abbots Langley and Bedmont. Thus the population is found either on the ridge or in the valleys near the rivers, the intermediate parts being dependent on water drawn from deep wells sunk into the chalk.

On the accompanying section (see next page), taken on the ridge midway between the rivers Gade and Ver, is shown the depth at which water is found, with its noted alternations at two periods in the same year. The level of the course of the river Gade, with which that of the Ver is nearly identical, is also given between these points. The surface of the subterranean water would be shown by an inclined line, fixed at the river, and more or less elevated or depressed towards the ridge according as the stock of water is augmented by the replenishment of the chalk stratum, or reduced by the natural drainage. Thus in chalk districts the level at which water is found may be accurately ascertained.

The intermediate space between the ridges, and the rivers which run in the valleys, is covered with gravel, often presenting a surface which consists almost entirely of flint-stones, the removal of which, if it were possible, would rather detract from, than add to the productiveness of the soil by quickening evaporation. This soil with slight variations forms the main staple of the district which lies between the outcrop of the London and Plastic clays and the northern limits of the county.

A stranger acquainted with those Western counties which have a soil almost identical with this in its texture and its geological bearings, is here struck by the absence of breeding flocks, the deficiency of stock, the inadequacy of the farm-buildings, and the small size of the enclosures which here prevail. He would find the land cleared of its sheep after the consumption of the swede and root-crop, the hay and straw very generally sold, and barely replaced by London manure, when it is to be had. Very many exceptions may of course be found, among which a farm at Wheathampstead, near the centre of the district under consideration, is a notable instance.

SHEEP FARM AT WHEATHAMPSTEAD.

The farm consists of 317 acres, of which 20 are in not very productive grass-land. Fifty-six acres of the arable are upon the strong loam of the higher levels, and the remainder is of a lighter

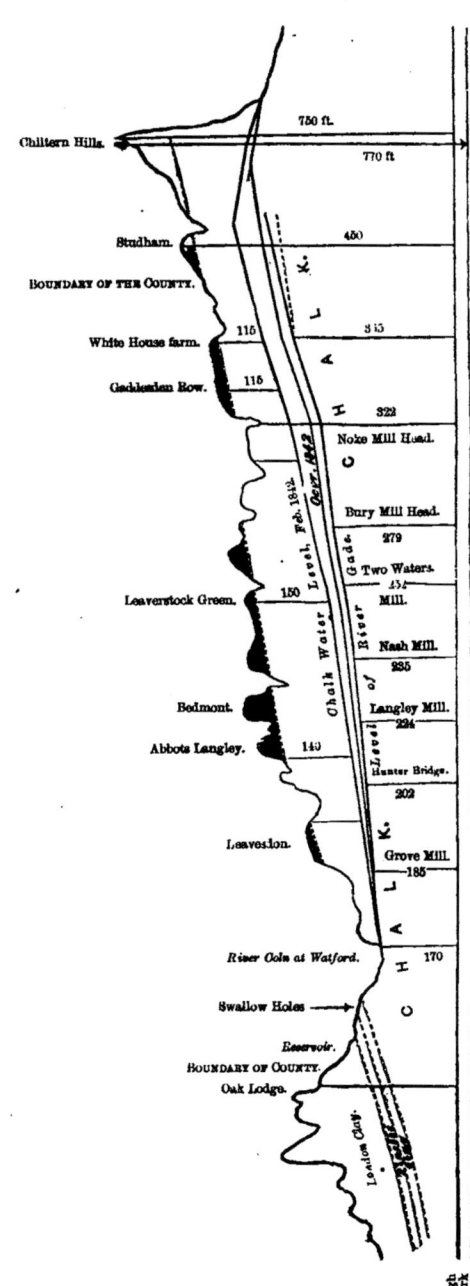

character—rather a sharp flint-gravel, somewhat under the average quality of the district. The whole has been more or less chalked from below, according to the custom of this county. The fertility of the farm is maintained, not by selling off the produce and trusting to London and other extraneous sources for an equivalent, but by developing and trusting to its own internal resources. The following list of animals fatted and sold from the farm has been kindly furnished in illustration of the system pursued:—

	1862.	1863.
Lambs	391	392
Sheep	333	356
Beasts	6	5
Calves	45	50
Pigs	205	198
Total head	980	1001

On 317 acres of land.

The system of cropping is four-course, managed with especial reference to sheep-stock. Much reliance is placed on the deep cultivation of the soil, which is principally effected by the use of a two-wheeled plough, divested of its mould-board, which follows the first plough, armed with a share copied from that of the unwieldy and disused old Hertfordshire plough. Besides the usual succession crops of swedes, mangold, mixed layers, tares (to be followed by white turnips), it is the practice here to sow rape between the rows of beans on the heavier portion of the farm.

A certain portion of the ewe flock, which averages 330 head, consists of Dorsets, which are put to a Sussex or half-bred ram; both ewe and lamb are generally fatted for sale, and the stock replenished from fairs.

The Chalk District.

The Northern or chalk district, having a fall anticlinal to the dip of the stratum, is drained by streamlets which are the affluents of the Cam, the Ouse, and, in one instance, of the Thame.

This remarkable tract of land may be surveyed looking from Sandon, which stands high on a rounded escarpment of the outlying Plastic clay.

On descending from the higher ground, the chalk—here geologically the lower chalk without flints—is more thinly covered with gravel, and very frequently becomes a part of the cultivated tilth. It does not, as in the Vales of Aylesbury and White Horse, end in bold escarpments immediately overhanging the upper green sand and gault, but sinks to the level of these strata by gentler undulations, which present a breadth of very useful arable land. This district is thus described by Sir Henry Chauncy in the 'Historical Antiquities of Hertfordshire' (1700) He says, "The Vale of Ringtale, or Wringtale, which lies north of the great ledge of hills crossing the northern part of this county (extending from Backway to Offley), where the soil is mixed with white marl, yields the choicest wheat and barley, such as makes the best mault that serves the King's Court or the City of London, which caused Queen Elizabeth often to boast of her Hitchin grape."

It has been noticed that this county comprehends within its boundary a small tract of land to the north of the villages of Ashwell and Caldicot, on the outcrop of the trace of the greensand and of the gault clay which underlies the lower chalk. It is all more or less covered by the drift of the chalk, though in some places the sheer gault lies very near the surface. Though its general features and management resemble those of the tract to the south just described, which rests on the lower chalk, there is this notable difference—that, as it rests on a clay subsoil, it requires thorough drainage. It was here that Mr. Bailey Denton carried out that mixed system of drainage of which there is so full and valuable a record in this Journal under the head of the Hinxworth Drainage.

Irrigation, Miils, and Meadows.

Although the streams which issue from the deep valleys by which the surface of the chalk is furrowed afford to this county abundant supplies of water, agriculturally they have not been turned to much account.

Near Rickmansworth, on the Chess, on the Bean, and at the Hoo, water-meadows indeed may be seen; but frequently the ancient weirs have been superseded by mills, the old water-rights having been either bought up by the millowner or lost by desuetude. The corn-mills themselves have often been diverted to the manufacture of paper, for which purpose machinery was first set up by M. Foudrienier, its inventor, on the river Gade.

The Gade, as its traverses this county, has a uniform fall of 14 feet per mile, which offers great natural facilities for irrigation, as well as water-power.

Drainage of Low Meadows.

Perhaps there is nothing in the whole county which more obviously calls for improvement than the so-called water-meadows, or rather marshy swamps, which line the banks of some of the rivers. This is more striking in districts where there is little natural or available grass-land. The remedy is simple. The mill-dams are impediments to the free action of the landowners, but very generally this difficulty may be overcome. The wetness of the meadows is not, even near the mill-heads, due to soakage from the river, but from stagnation in the soil of water derived from springs on either side of the valleys. As a remedy, first a ditch should be cut as near to the side of the valley and as far from the river as possible. In some cases pipes of large bore might be used; the spring-water should then be led below the outfall provided by the next mill-dam; the cleansing of the ditches, brick-rubbish, or any hard material, should be placed or even piled on the surface of the meadows; then with ordinary attention to keeping up the river-banks and filling up all transverse ditches, much valuable land might be reclaimed from its virtual sterility.

WATER-CRESSES.

A new rival to the water-meadow has sprung up of late from the artificial culture of water-cresses. Fifty years ago those who sold this plant were content "to strip the brook with mantling cresses spread." One such was Mr. Bradbury, to whom the idea suggested itself that water-cresses might be cultivated to advantage. He obtained permission first to try the experiment in spring-ditches at West Hyde, in the parish of Rickmansworth, just on the borders of Bucks, and satisfied the occupier of the land that the cleansing of the ditches and regulation of the height of the water in them as practised by Mr. Bradbury was beneficial. The ditches were next let at a certain rent and under certain restrictions, and very shortly Bradbury's cultivated watercresses became a regular article of traffic in the London market. From this small beginning a large trade has sprung up, which now extends to the Manufacturing Districts. The persons who hire the spring-ditches for the cultivation of the plant scour and cleanse them with much care, level their bottoms, and often expand their area till they form a series of shallow lakes, in which the height of the water is regulated by dams. These dams are either permanent—formed of stones or two lines of boards, supported by stakes, between which clay is rammed; or temporary—consisting of moveable boards, bricks, or other materials. These, in some cases, are either placed transversely to the flow of the water, to keep it to its required level in the subdivisions of the beds, or else so arranged that the stream may be conducted under the bank-side, apart from the adjacent bed, as by an irrigation-carrier, to any spot below. Very frequently borings are made in the chalk to facilitate the issue of the clear spring-water in its purity, which is deemed of great importance to the quality of the crop. The best sorts of cresses are then selected, that most in request is known as the Dutch Brown, from the shade of colour it takes when it has reached maturity. The plants are placed in rows, generally with stones upon them, to prevent their being removed by the flow of the water. All this is done at considerable expense; besides which it is necessary to guard the beds from attacks of birds, especially the blackbird, whose ravages at certain seasons are of a very serious character. By regulating the height of the water in the various divisions a proper succession in the ripening of the crop is secured. The cutting is performed either by wading in waterproof boots between the rows, or by placing moveable planks across the beds. The washing and packing in hampers or baskets finishes the operation. The growth of this simple and indigenous plant is daily on the increase; the letting the ditches for this purpose is more profitable to the landowner than the irrigation of the meadows, if it could be done; the rent cannot be estimated by the acreage under cultivation. Such sums as 40*l.*, 50*l.*, and upwards are often paid by persons who have little capital but their industry, and employ a great proportionate amount of other labour in gaining their living.

Cherry-Orchards.

In the western parts of the county the cherry-orchards occupy so considerable a portion of the soil, and form so great an item in the rural economy, as to demand attention. They are generally found at a high elevation, where there is a considerable depth of loam, clay, or gravel, naturally drained by the chalk beneath. The great age of many of the trees shows that their culture is of ancient date, as also appears from the agricultural histories of Hertfordshire. It does not seem that these orchards have been extended of late years, in spite of the access to the Manufacturing Districts afforded by the introduction of railways. The great drawback to the cultivation is the precarious nature of the crop, which is very often destroyed in a single night by an untimely frost, apart from other casualties to which fruit-crops are liable. The fruit is generally sold on the trees to dealers, and realises from 12*s.* to 16*s.* per "ped" or basket, holding about four dozen pounds. The sorts grown, though not confined to the county, are characteristic of Hertfordshire. These are known as the Caroon, the largest sort, and small Hertfordshire black. Besides the usual uses, they are converted into cherry brandy, and, if report says true, enter very largely into the composition of other liquors, to which they do not give their name. They are also used for the purpose of dyeing.

Woods and Plantations.

Woodlands cover a large part of the surface of this county. The quantity and quality of timber varies considerably in different districts. In the north-western portion, where the chalk is near the surface, beech woods prevail. To the south of this, on a zone running from the south-west to north-east, oak and ash are more abundant, both in the woods and on hedge rows, the oak having generally a stunted appearance; the ash is also of slow growth, but bears a good character for wheeler's stuff. Still further south the elm may be said to be the weed of the country. In the most southern portion, where the chalk is covered by the London and Plastic clays, the elm and oak attain a much larger growth, unless the upper drift gravel intervene, which is only suited to larch or fir. The beech woods, in which underwood refuses to grow, are periodically thinned, and the fall used by wheelers, and, in some cases, by chair-makers, though this trade is almost entirely confined to Buckinghamshire. The ordinary coppice is commonly cut every twelve years and sold by auction. As a general rule, the growth is not sufficiently straight and free to serve a better purpose than making rods or headers for fencing, pea-sticks, faggots, or at best, turner's stuff, or sparred hurdles and wattled hurdles for sheep.

The woodlands are too often objects of little care, and are scarcely ever renewed or replanted as the old stools die or fail. Those which belonged to the late Sir John Sebright, of Beechwood, are, however, an exception to this rule, and bear the traces of careful replenishing to this day; his son and successor follows his example.

In many places woods have of late been grubbed, when, from their frequent interlacing with the arable land, they were incompatible with improved cultivation; but in a county where there are so many resident proprietors, coverts for game will not readily give place to the steam plough.

Straw-Plait.

The manufacture of straw-plait not only furnishes employment for the females of the labouring classes, but bears on the agricultural interests of part of the county, by creating a market for some of the wheat-straw grown within its limits. This trade, from its nature, varies with and is ruled by the fashions in dress. Luton and Dunstable, in Bedfordshire, are its headquarters, though it extends to the centre of the county of Hertford, where much plait is made to supply the dealers, whose attendance at Hitchin and elsewhere creates a considerable market. The straw grown on the chalk soils at the north of the county is well fitted for the purpose. The straw drawers either purchase the straw in the bulk, and take away all that suits their purpose, or, more commonly, bargain to take, by weight, that only which they select. The farmer who has a crop fitted for the purpose has it reaped with great care, if the weather be fine, in an early stage of its maturity, leaving the sheaves open for a time till they are quite dry, and setting aside those in which the straw may be twisted; they are then placed, with care, in the rick or mow, so as to come out quite straight and uninjured. The person who is employed by the dealer to draw the straw takes a certain quantity from the sheaf and binds it quite tight with a leathern strap; he then places his parcel, thus formed, between his legs, takes a few straws at a time just beneath the ears and draws them out, until his other hand, to which he transfers them, is full, and ties the handful, like a gleaner, beneath the ears. The flag is removed by a coarse iron-toothed comb, the ears are cut off, and it is then handed to a second person, who makes up bundles about a foot in diameter, neatly bound with straw. The straw is then in a marketable state, and passes to the manufacturer to be sorted, cut into lengths, and so fitted for use. The waste is not so great as might be supposed, all the chaff and caving is left behind with the ears, and with much of the rough straw, which may be converted into manure. The operation puts the farmer to some inconvenience, but the price given is remunerative, amounting, on an average, to about a penny per pound, so that the value of the straw may exceed that of the corn.

The moral effects of this manufacture are often called in question; the early age at which the children are employed sadly hinders their education by keeping them from the village school; it indisposes and unfits them for domestic service, though it retains them at home and hinders their being subjected to the drudgery of field labour.

Varieties of Wheat.

Although the vale of Ringtale, in the north of the county, gained a name of old for the Hertfordshire white flour, the land generally is better adapted to the coarser red wheats, and high farming cannot in this respect overrule the inherent quality of the soil.

To Mr. Hainworth, of Hitchin, great credit is due for the attention bestowed by him on the selection and improvement of wheats. He is a cultivator of Spalding, Syer's Red, Red Straw White, Hopetown White, Red Lammas, and other wheats; and has given his own name to a variety raised by him from a single ear, which he specially recommends, as bearing the forcing of high farming.

As the fair testing of different sorts of wheat on the same ground is as difficult as it is important, Mr. Hainworth's method is worthy of notice. First he selects a field in which the soil is as near as may be, of an uniform character, measuring, for example, 16 poles wide by 33 poles long; 8 rows of each different sort of wheat are dibbled with great care, the short way of the land, 9 inches apart, and 5 inches between the holes, in each of which three corns are deposited. This is repeated in succession until the whole piece of land is cropped with say 11 beds of each sort. The 8 rows of each variety in each bed are reaped separately, bound and set up, then brought together, threshed and measured, thus giving a fair average of the whole 11 beds, grown in different parts of the same field. The farm on which these experiments are made is necessarily in a high and cleanly state of cultivation; its fertility, in fact, is maintained by the application of London stable manure. If this careful selection, cultivation, and testing of varieties of wheat be looked on merely as a commercial speculation, the results must be valuable; but in this case, as in almost all such, the higher object of advancing the interests of agriculture gives a fresh stimulus to the labour and skill which such experiments at all times require.

Sheep.

After a word of commendation of the Hoo flock of 400 Sussex downs, improved of late by rams from Babraham, and a word of warning as to the ultimate results of cross-breeding between the long and short woolled races, however promising at first, I pass on to speak of that which for not less than two centuries has been called "the far-famed Bennington flock." Bennington is a village near the centre of the county, between Stevenage and Standon. The flock, which is still owned by the descendants of those who first formed it, is said to have sprung originally from the old Wiltshire horned breed, which appears to have formed the staple of the sheep stock in the midland counties of England up to the beginning of the present century. Within the memory of many persons, the horn, one of its distinguishing features, though reduced in size, was still retained, and in all respects the sheep were nearer their original type than at present. Attempts at improvements were at one time made by the introduction of Leicester, Gloucester, or Cotswold rams, though the produce of one, if not both these crosses, was weeded from the flock. Of late years the chief, if not the only new blood, has been Lincoln; some of the flock still retain traces of the Roman nose, and other traits which render this flock remarkable, both as a record of the past, and a most interesting instance of the successful breeding of long woolled sheep. It is said, and the assertion is borne out by the appearance, great size, and noble character of the flock, that the weight to which the ewes attain when fatted is 20 stone, that a teg has been known to shear 21¾ lb. of wool; and that the average weight of two fleeces is 28 lb., or 1 tod. The flock now unfortunately numbers only 200. The value placed on them for breeding purposes may be learned by the significant fact, that all the ram lambs are saved, and command a ready sale at good prices.

It may be a question whether this breed and quality of sheep is that best fitted to a neighbourhood and soil such as that on which it has been so long and so successfully maintained; the mere fact of its existence, however, supplies an argument in its favour. They are said to do better and to be more hardy than the Lincolns, by which, from time to time, the stock has been replenished, and compared this year favourably with some Lincolns newly imported, which stood beside them in the fold.

IMPLEMENTS.

One novelty among implements is to be found in the adjustment of shafts for the purpose of turning, or rather reversing the action of a heavy iron roller, an unpatented invention of the owner of Beechwood, which weighs 3 tons, and can be loaded by filling a cradle with stones up to 4 tons. The roller is used either on the sward of the park, or to compress the roads; in either case, the difficulty is to turn so heavy an implement with two horses drawing abreast, and necessarily leaning on a shaft. This is avoided by fitting the double shaft to the upper of two hollow discs of woodwork encircling the cylinder, which revolves after the manner of a railway turn-table on that beneath it. For the purpose of turning, two vertical iron pins, by which the discs are fastened together, are drawn, the horses make a half turn, the pins are replaced, and the roller is ready to move in the opposite direction, without the least strain or inconvenience to the team.

Printed by Libri Plureos GmbH in Hamburg, Germany